JUDY'S RAGGEDY ANN

Written by
Donald Dentinger

Illustrated by
Carrie Lantz

Once upon a time there lived a very old rag doll. Like most rag dolls, her name was Ann. Ann lived in a beautiful, stone house.

Ann came to live in the stone house many years ago. She was new—so clean and bright. Her cheeks were red, the color of fresh strawberries. Her two shanks of auburn hair were neatly braided. She had a cute little nose, like a shiny button. Ann's big blue eyes matched the checks in her lovely gingham dress.

Ann wore a cheerful smile on her face.

Ann belonged to Judy. Judy was the oldest of two daughters who lived in the large stone house. Ann was given to Judy on her first birthday.

Judy loved her rag doll very dearly. Ann always slept in Judy's bed. Judy talked with her rag doll, and even spoke to Ann about her deepest secrets. Each night, Judy would tell Ann a bedtime story—kiss her goodnight, and then hug her rag doll closely, until she awoke the next morning.

If Judy went for a walk with her mother,
she always took Ann with her.

Sometimes, she went for a ride with Judy in her father's big, shiny car.

Judy even took Ann to the old gray Church where her family worshipped every Sunday.

Judy took good care of her rag doll. In return, Ann loved Judy very much.

After Judy was old enough, she started school. Judy missed Ann during school hours. And after a time, she became so busy with her school work and new friends, Judy had hardly any time to spend with her rag doll.

One day after school, Judy took Ann into her younger sister's room.

"I have a present for you," Judy told her sister. "I have little time to spend with Ann. She might be lonely, with no one to play with. I want you to have her."

"Take very good care of Ann—she's a wonderful friend..." Judy added, as she handed the rag doll to her sister.

But, Judy's little sister did not take good care of the rag doll. Once, she left Ann outside all night. It rained very hard. Ann's strawberry cheeks faded. Her face and dress were covered with mud.

Another time, the little sister spoke very harshly to Ann. Ann could not imagine what she had done wrong, but Judy's sister was quite angry. She grabbed Ann and threw her down, very hard, on the floor of the bedroom. The poor rag doll's leg split open, and one of her eyes was badly damaged.

Ann hurt so much. She cried little tears of sawdust every day, thereafter.

To make matters even worse, a new puppy was given to the family. The puppy loved to grab Ann with her little sharp teeth, dragging her around the house.

One day, the puppy was chewing on Ann's toes. The pain was awful. The little dog kept gnawing—until he was pulling rags out of one of Ann's toes.

Judy rescued her from the puppy, just in
the nick of time. Judy put most of the rag
stuffing back. And then, Judy decided that
Ann needed a good hiding place—somewhere
Ann would be safe from the puppy.

Judy took Ann upstairs to the attic. She put the rag doll on an old rocking chair with broken arms. Before turning off the light, Judy promised Ann that she would return for her when it was safe to bring her back downstairs.

Ann lived in the cold, dark attic for many years. Each day, she waited patiently for Judy to return. She had no one to talk to. Ann was very lonely.

Her only companions were a near-sighted mouse and two spiders. Ann had always been afraid of mice. She worried constantly that the little mouse would nibble her toes or fingers while she was asleep.

The spiders were no better companions. They were interesting to watch, but all they ever did was spin their webs all over the attic room. They were too busy, and too quiet.

As each year passed, Ann's face grew thin from having spent so many nights crying her little tears of sawdust.

Then, one evening, Ann heard footsteps on the attic stairs. The door opened. The light snapped on brightly—nearly blinding Ann.

Ann recognized one of the voices. It was Judy! And, Judy was talking to a little girl.

Brushing cobwebs away, Judy made her way toward the old rocking chair where she had put Ann, so many years ago.

Ann looked up at them. Judy was much older. Ann could hardly recognize her. The little girl with her, however, looked exactly like Judy.

Judy spoke to her daughter. "This is Ann. She was my best friend when I was a little girl. I want you and Ann to become good friends, too."

"But, Mommy..." The little girl looked disappointed.

"Don't worry about how sad and miserable Ann looks," Judy told her daughter. "We will give Ann a nice warm bath...and after she's all cleaned up, my needle and thread will make her look just like new."

Judy took Ann downstairs. After she put her daughter to bed, Judy washed the dirt and dust off. Ann's strawberry complexion and cheerful smile began to return. She carefully sewed up the rag doll's leg. She sewed Ann's little button nose on tightly, and fixed Ann's eye. Then, Judy made a new dress and put it on Ann. It fit perfectly.

"My, how pretty you look" Judy told Ann after she had finished.

The next morning, Judy gave the rag doll to her daughter.

"I can't believe how pretty Ann is!"
the little girl told her mother.

Then, Judy's daughter smiled at Ann, and she took her into her room to play. As you might imagine, Ann and her new friend lived happily ever after.

The End